Archway Publishing books may be ordered through booksellers or by contacting:

Archway Publishing
1663 Liberty Drive
Bloomington, IN 47403
www.archwaypublishing.com
844-669-3957

Interior Image Credit: Dana Scott

ISBN: 978-1-6657-6472-8 (sc)
ISBN: 978-1-6657-6473-5 (e)

Library of Congress Control Number: 2024916911

Print information available on the last page.

Archway Publishing rev. date: 10/02/2024

ARCHWAY
PUBLISHING

Hello my name is Shibby, I'm a heifer cow, how cool is that? I'm so happy to be a heifer cow, and I love taking my naps in the warm afternoon sun. It's so peaceful and calm, and I feel so happy. I'm so lucky to be able to enjoy such a wonderful experience here on our little farm.

Here is Fefe, our beloved little bunny! How we love watching her relax and take her sleepy little naps. Those cozy moments of snuggling up and blissful slumber are such a treat for us all! We can't help but smile when we see her snoozing away. She gets to enjoy some peaceful downtime. Fefe certainly deserves quiet time.

Our lovely ducks are so content when they get to rest in the cool shade, on the soft wood shavings. It's the best place for them to take a break from the warm summer weather. They just love it! Our ducks are so cute!

Brittany is always looking out for me! This morning she woke me up bright and early to make sure we had plenty of time to get ready for our trip to the beach. She's so thoughtful and caring. I really appreciate all she does for me! She is the best.

I enjoy my really big bucket of cool water that I drink from, I also enjoy scratching my nose along the edge. I'm so lucky to have such a big bucket of water. It's wonderful to have something so big and reliable to turn to when I'm really thirsty.

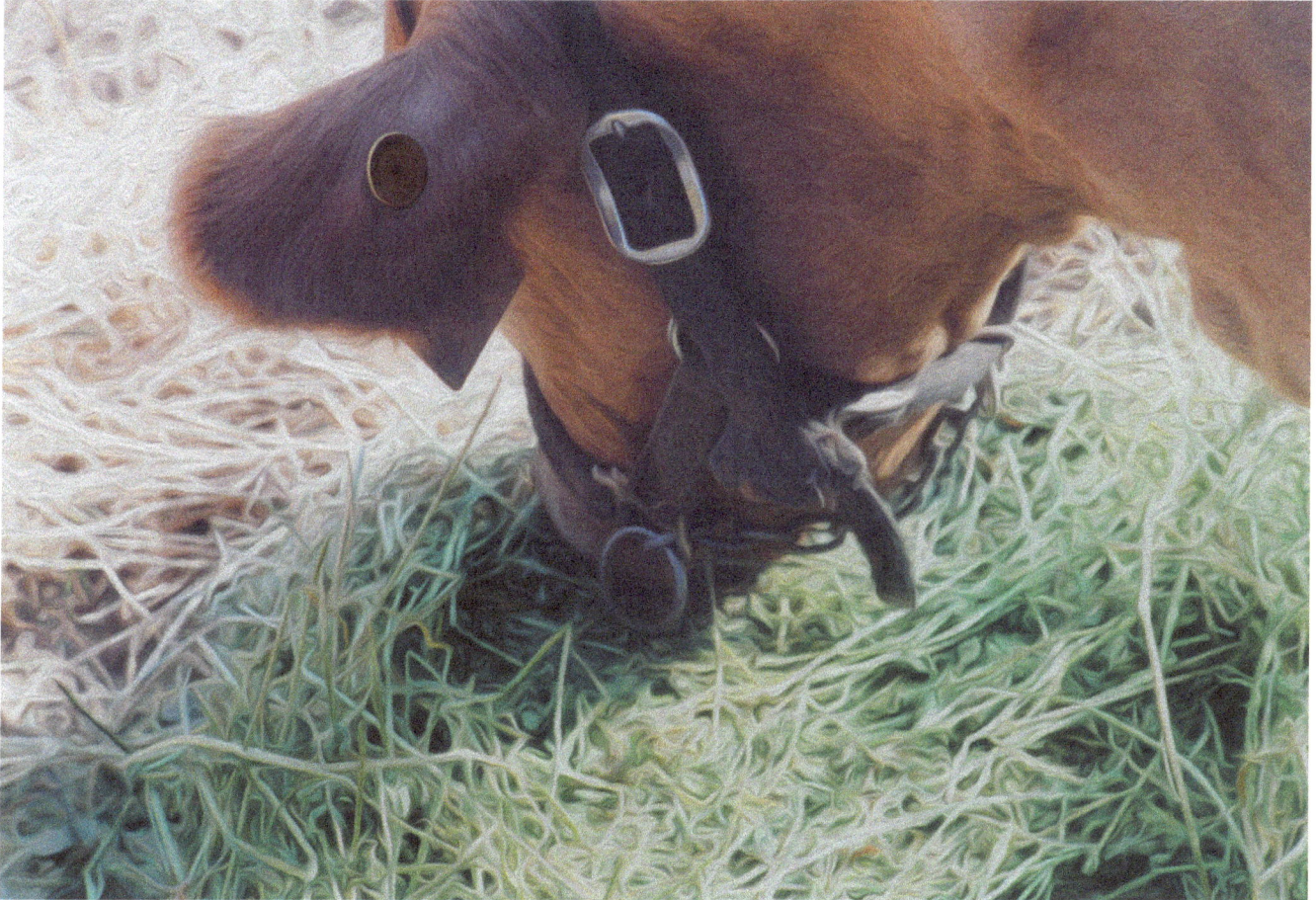

Before our trip to the beach I like to munch on some fresh alfalfa too. Did you know that sometimes alfalfa is called hay? My alfalfa is fresh and fragrant, it smells so good and it's delicious.

I am kind of really excited now to get this trip going! I get to ride in our livestock trailer, this is going to be so much fun! I'm ready to go see the beach, let's go!

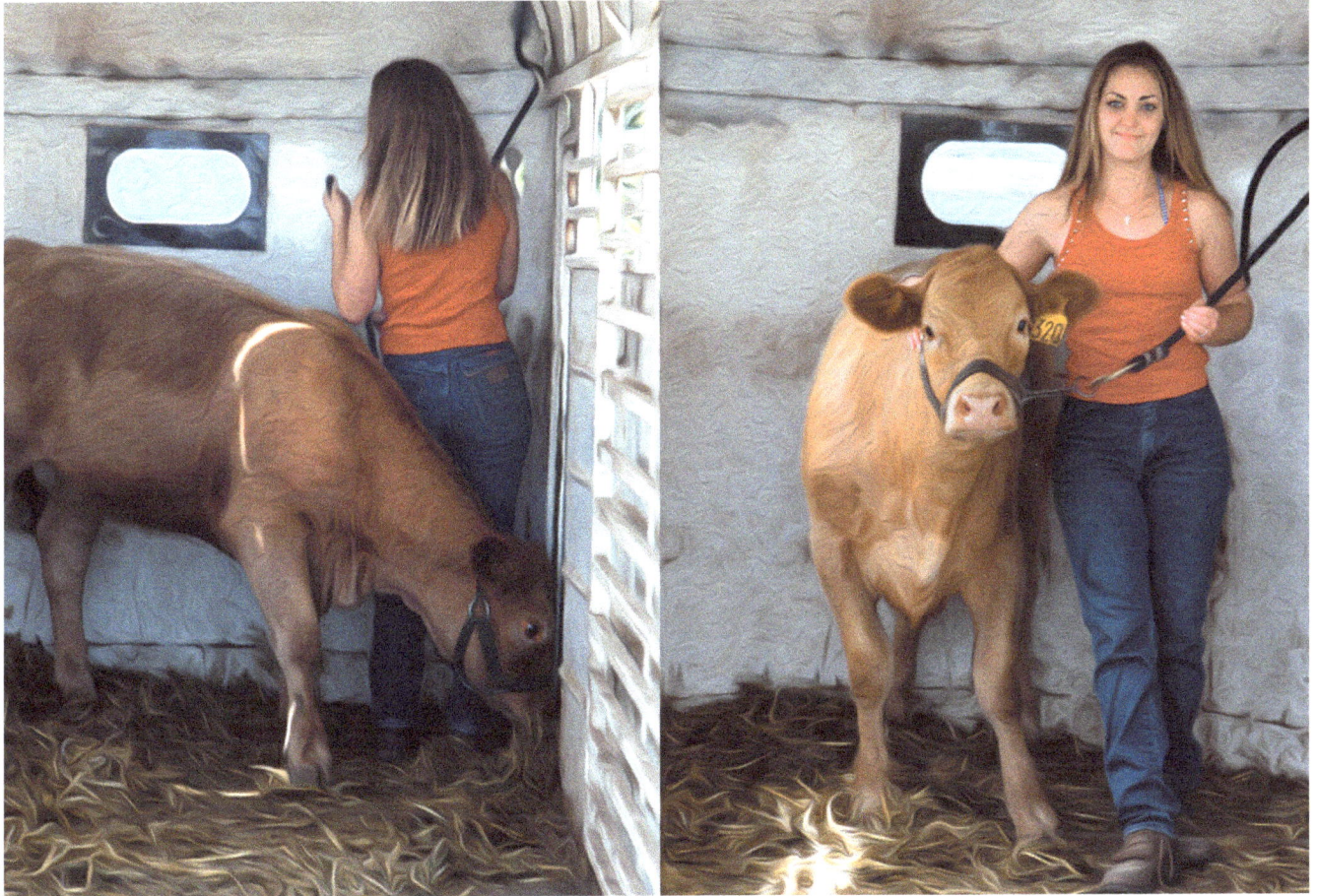

Brittany safely attached my halter on-board our livestock trailer. I can't wait to explore the beach with her. I'm sure it will be a cool adventure, I am really ready now. Our livestock trailer makes it fun, easy and safe.

Brittany made sure I was extra safe by locking the safety bars in place inside the trailer. I felt a sense of comfort knowing that she had taken the extra step to make sure I was safe and secure. It was nice to know our livestock trailer has the safety bars. This is kind of like wearing your seatbelt, keeping me safe while we ride down to the beach.

Finally we are at the beach, and it's a short walk around the corner from where we parked our livestock trailer. I can see the beach from here, wow this is so exciting! Mr. Avila, our Agriculture Teacher from our High School was helping us too, he is really fun and is an excellent teacher.

The kids at the beach could not believe we were walking out towards the sand. We stopped and said hello. They got to know us a little bit by asking my name. They were really nice to us, very complementary. We were all so excited to be there, and it was a great feeling to be able to share that moment together.

As we stopped the kids could take a closer, longer look. Well I thought to myself, it is not too often you see a cow like me walking onto the beach. They were very kind, and said I was really cool! Wow how nice. I think they were pretty cool kids!

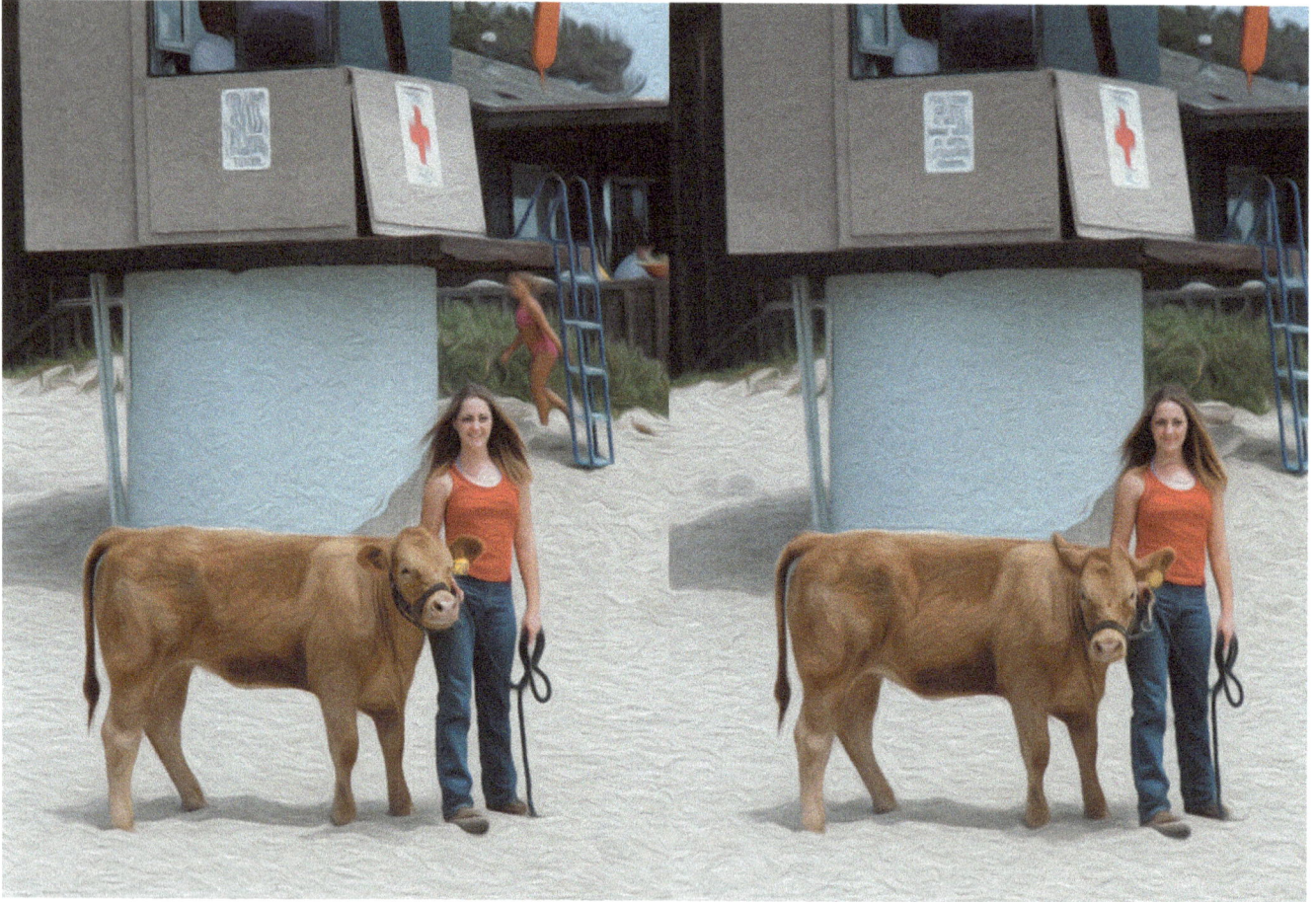

As we walked onto the sand we decided it was best to ask the lifeguard on duty up in the tower if it was okay for us to be on the beach. He said yes it was okay with a big smile, he was pretty excited too. I like both of these pictures, which one do you like?

I couldn't believe my eyes when I saw the big green tractor parked in the sand. The city of Carpinteria uses the tractor to help keep the sand nice and clean for everybody, explained Mr. Avila our High School Agriculture Teacher. He also wanted to take pictures of us next to the tractor. I was not too sure about that at first. However once we got up close, this tractor looked most interesting parked at the beach, it was a John Deere tractor, we thought it looked pretty good. It reminded me of our farm.

At first I didn't want to get too close to the tractor. However Brittany said it would be fine and I don't need to worry about it. Mr. Avila helped by pushing me closer so we could take a good looking picture next to the tractor.

Once we got up close, I thought wow this looked interesting. The tractor is the perfect background for taking pictures. I smiled and looked at the camera. I think I look beautiful in this photograph.

Will you look at me? Here I am in a close up picture. I was really proud to stand next to the tractor with Brittany. She was so sweet to take me to the beach, I just love it here. I think I am a very beautiful heifer too!

I really think this is my very best picture, all of me and the good looking John Deere tractor next to me. Okay, this is my selfie! What do you think?

We started walking down toward the water, and I stopped. I really did not want to go into the water. Brittany said not to worry as she pulled on my halter. I was still very cautious. But I really did want to walk along the water where the waves were splashing along the beach.

How nice it was to walk along the beach with Brittany! It was a beautiful day! What fun we had together. I really love the beach. It's was a really nice idea to bring me here! Thank you Brittany.

Our teacher Mr. Avila was having fun too, he enjoyed our little trip! At our school, we are in an organization called the Future Farmers of America, we simply call it the FFA. What a wonderful program for Brittany and I, we learned all about farming, and leadership in agriculture.

It was getting late in the day, it was time for us to head back to our livestock trailer for the ride back to our farm.

It was a short trip from the beach back to the farm. When we got out of the livestock trailer I was happy to be home.

Fefe our bunny was excited that we were back on the farm. She jumped up to take a closer look. She never misses any activity.

After walking around on the beach and posing for all of our pictures, and riding in our livestock trailer I was really thirsty. The cool water was just perfect for me.

Brittany just filled up my big feed bucket. It was dinner time and yes I was hungry. I was ready for dinner, OK let's eat!

I like to eat my dinner out of my big feed trough. It is kind of like a really big bowl.

Fefe eats with me about the same time. She enjoys eating fresh apple and lettuce with her small bowl of water.

Our ducks waddled out onto the grass yard to see what we were up to. They like to munch on bugs and snails in addition to their regular feed. We really love our ducks, they are a big part of our family.

After a busy day at the beach, I was very tired. It was time to relax. I am just about ready to go to sleep.

Later that month at our local County Fair Livestock Competition, I was awarded the First Place Blue Ribbon Award as the Reserve Grand Champion! That was so much fun and very important to me! Once in a while I also love scratching my chin on our ranch style farm fence.

9 781665 764728